Reteach:
Phonics Skills
Level 1
Blackline Masters

A Division of The **McGraw·Hill** Companies

Columbus, Ohio

www.sra4kids.com

SRA/McGraw-Hill

A Division of The McGraw·Hill Companies

Send all inquiries to:
SRA/McGraw-Hill
8787 Orion Place
Columbus, OH 43240-4027

Printed in the United States of America.

ISBN 0-07-572034-5

2 3 4 5 6 7 8 9 POH 07 06 05 04 03 02

Table of Contents

Name _____ Date _____

▶Writing Letters

PHONICS SKILLS

Directions: Trace the first two letters and write three more letters on the lines.

Copyright © SRA/McGraw-Hill. Permission is granted to reproduce this page for classroom use.

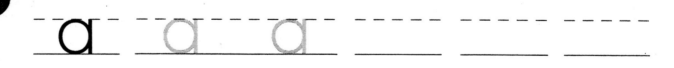

Letter Knowledge • **Reteach: Phonics Skills**

UNIT 1   Let's Read! • **Lesson 2** *The Purple Cow*

▶ Writing Letters

Directions: Trace the first two letters and write three more letters on the lines.

PHONICS SKILLS

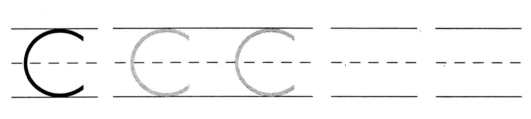

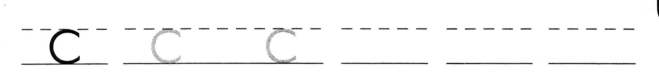

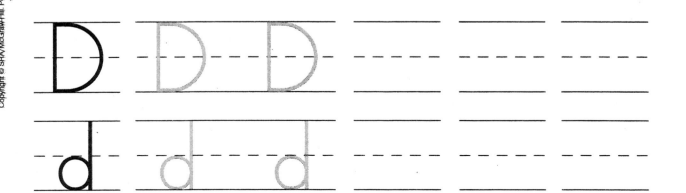

Name _____ Date _____

▶ Writing Letters

Directions: Trace the first two letters and write three more letters on the lines.

PHONICS SKILLS

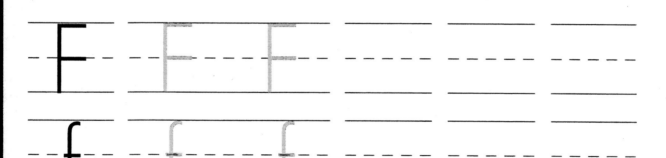

Name _____ Date _____

▶ Writing Letters

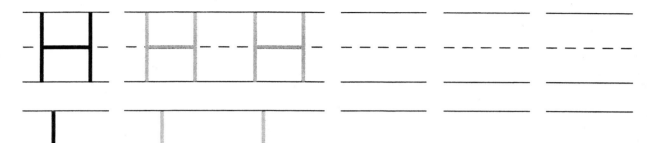

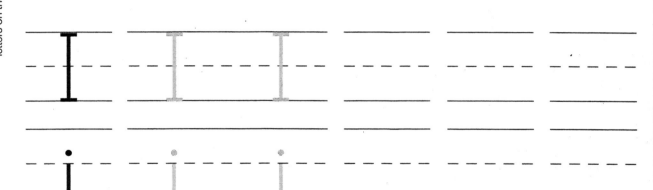

PHONICS SKILLS

UNIT 1   Let's Read! • **Lesson 5** *Hey, Diddle, Diddle*

▶ Writing Letters

Directions: Trace the first two letters and write three more letters on the lines.

PHONICS SKILLS

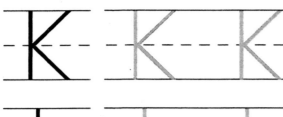

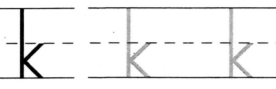

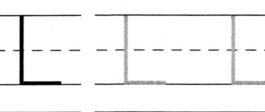

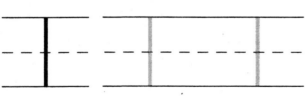

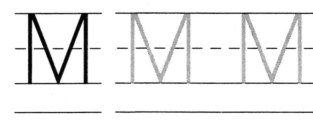

▶ Writing Letters

Directions: Trace the first two letters and write three more letters on the lines.

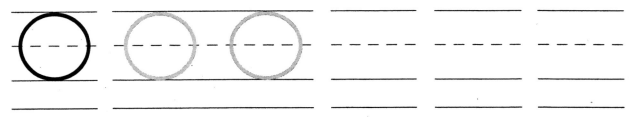

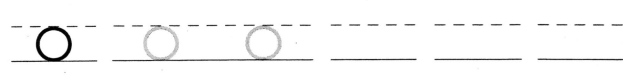

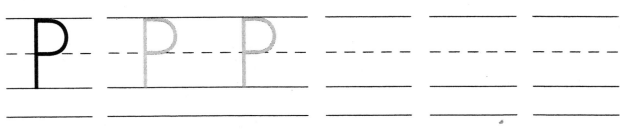

PHONICS SKILLS

Name _____ Date _____

▶ Writing Letters

Directions: Trace the first two letters and write three more letters on the lines.

PHONICS SKILLS

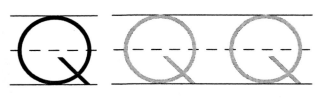

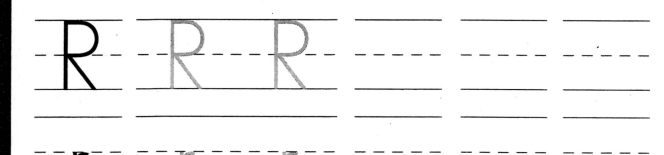

Letter Knowledge • Reteach: Phonics Skills

Name _____ Date _____

▶ Writing Letters

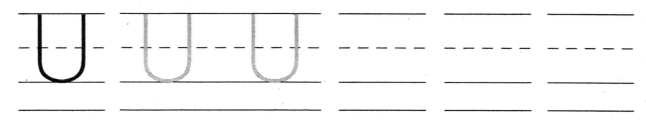

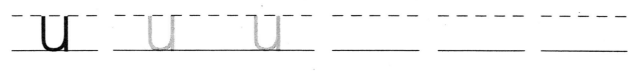

PHONICS SKILLS

▶ Writing Letters

Directions: Trace the first two letters and write three more letters on the lines.

Copyright © SRA/McGraw-Hill. Permission is granted to reproduce this page for classroom use.

PHONICS SKILLS

Name _____ Date _____

▶ Writing Letters

PHONICS SKILLS

UNIT 1   Let's Read! • **Lesson 10** *Twinkle Twinkle Firefly*

▶ Capital and Lowercase Letters

PHONICS SKILLS

a b c d e f g h i j k l m n o p q r s t u v w x y z
A B C D E F G H I J K L M N O P Q R S T U V W X Y Z

a •   b •   c •   d •   e •   f •    g •

J •   K •   L •   M •   N •   O •   P •

   H •   I •

   q •   r •   s •   t •   u •   v •   w •   x •   y •   z •

Capital and Lowercase Letters • Reteach: Phonics Skills

UNIT 1 Let's Read! • **Lesson 10** *Twinkle Twinkle Firefly*

▶ Capital and Lowercase Letters

a b c d e f g h i j k l m n o p q r s t u v w x y z
A B C D E F G H I J K L M N O P Q R S T U V W X Y Z

Directions: Connect the dots in order.

PHONICS SKILLS

B C
A   D E F
G

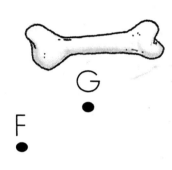

h n
i k m o
j l p

Q R
S T U V W Y
X
Z

Name _____ Date _____

▶ Sounds and Spellings

PHONICS SKILLS

S

S

S

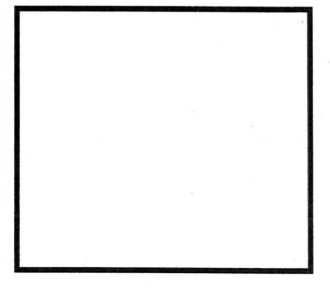

Sounds and Spellings • Reteach: Phonics Skills

▶ Sounds and Spellings

Directions: Say the name of the picture. Write a capital S next to each picture that begins with the /s/ sound.

 _____

 _____

 _____

 _____

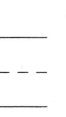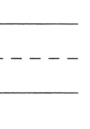 _____

 _____

PHONICS SKILLS

UNIT 1   Let's Read! • **Lesson 12** *The Chase*

▶Sounds and Spellings

PHONICS SKILLS

m

m

M

UNIT 1 Let's Read! • **Lesson 12** *The Chase*

▶ Sounds and Spellings

PHONICS SKILLS

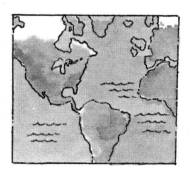

Name _____ Date _____

▶ Sounds and Spellings

PHONICS SKILLS

a

a

A

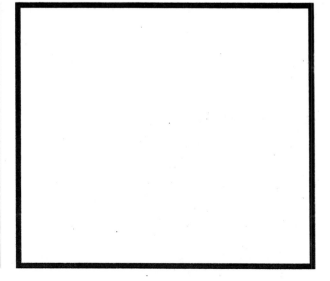

Name _____ Date _____

▶ Reading and Writing

PHONICS SKILLS

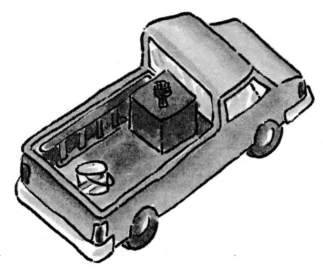

I am in the

I am on the

I am a _____.

I am in the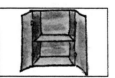

I am on the

I am a _____.

UNIT 1   Let's Read! • **Lesson 14** *Mrs. Goose's Baby*

▶ Sounds and Spellings

Directions: Practice writing *t* and *T*. Copy the word on the line. Then draw two pictures whose names begin with the /t/ sound.

PHONICS SKILLS

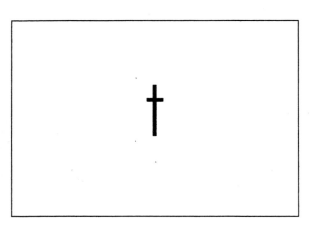

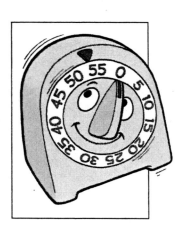

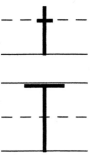

sat

Sounds and Spellings • Reteach: **Phonics Skills**

UNIT 1 Let's Read! • **Lesson 14** *Mrs. Goose's Baby*

▶ Sounds and Spellings

_____
- - - - - - - - - -
_____

_____
- - - - - - - - - -
_____

PHONICS SKILLS

_____
- - - - - - - - - -
_____

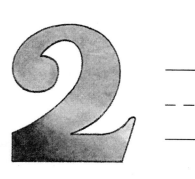

_____
- - - - - - - - - -
_____

_____
- - - - - - - - - -
_____

UNIT 1 Let's Read! • **Lesson 15** *Babybuggy*

▶Sounds and Spellings

Directions: Practice writing *h* and *H*. Then draw two pictures whose names begin with the /h/ sound. .

PHONICS SKILLS

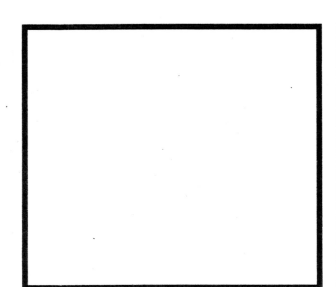

UNIT I Let's Read! • **Lesson 15** *Babybuggy*

▶ Sounds and Spellings

 _____

 _____

 _____

 _____

 _____

PHONICS SKILLS

UNIT 2   Animals • **Lesson 1** *Unit Introduction*

▶Sounds and Spellings

Directions: Practice writing *p* and *P*. Copy the word. Then, draw two pictures whose names begin with the /p/ sound.

PHONICS SKILLS

p

p
p

pat _ _ _ _ _ _

UNIT 2 Animals • **Lesson I** *Unit Introduction*

▶ Decoding

Pam has sap.
Pam has a mat.

I tap the map.
I pat the hat.

Pat has a tam.
Pat has a ham.

_____

- -

_____

PHONICS SKILLS

UNIT 2 **Animals • Lesson 2** *Raccoons*

▶ Sounds and Spellings

Directions: Practice writing *i* and *I*. Copy the word. Then, draw two pictures whose names have the /i/ sound.

PHONICS SKILLS

i

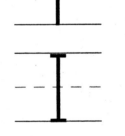

sit

Name _____ Date _____

▶ Writing Words

PHONICS SKILLS

t _ _ i _ _ p

Name _____ Date _____

▶Sounds and Spellings

Directions: Practice writing *n* and *N*. Copy the word. Then, draw two pictures whose names begin with the /n/ sound.

PHONICS SKILLS

n

n

N

nip

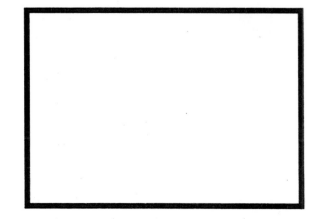

Sounds and Spellings • Reteach: Phonics Skills

Name _____ Date _____

UNIT 2 Animals • **Lesson 3** *Baby Animals*

▶ Decoding

Directions: Look at the pictures and circle the correct word to finish each sentence. Write the correct word for the last two.

Copyright © SRA/McGraw-Hill. Permission is granted to reproduce this page for classroom use.

Nan has a _____.

pan
pin

I am a _____.

man
map

It is an _____.

mat
ant

Tim has a _____.

ham
pan

PHONICS SKILLS

Reteach: Phonics Skills • *Decoding*

UNIT 2 • Lesson 3 **29**

Name _____ Date _____

▶Sounds and Spellings

Directions: Practice writing *l* and *L*. Copy the word. Then, draw two pictures whose names begin with the /l/ sound.

lap _____

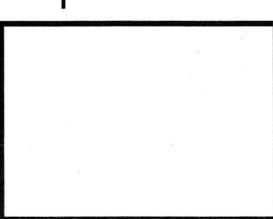

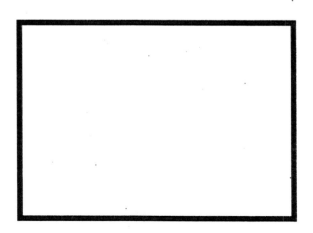

PHONICS SKILLS

Sounds and Spellings • Reteach: Phonics Skills

UNIT 2 Animals • **Lesson 4** *Baby Animals*

▶Decoding

PHONICS SKILLS

list

lamp

hill

pals

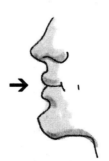

lips

Name _____ Date _____

Directions: Write the correct word for each picture.

Copyright © SRA/McGraw-Hill. Permission is granted to reproduce this page for classroom use.

▶Review

PHONICS SKILLS

hit	lamp	ant	pan

_____

- - - - - - - - - - - - - -

_____

_____

- - - - - - - - - - - - - -

_____

_____

- - - - - - - - - - - - - -

_____

_____

- - - - - - - - - - - - - -

_____

▶Review

The ant is on a _____.

| pan |
| pin |

Lil has a _____.

| mitt |
| map |

PHONICS SKILLS

Tim has a _____.
_____
- - - - - - - - -

| hill |
| hat |

Name _____ Date _____

▶Sounds and Spellings

Directions: Practice writing *d* and *D*. Copy the word. Then, draw two pictures whose names begin with the /d/ sound.

PHONICS SKILLS

d

d

D

did _ _ _ _ _ _ _

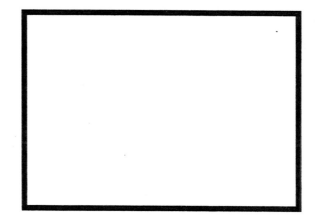

▷Reading and Writing

sad
had

did
pad

Dad had a nap.
Dad hid the hat.

_____

_ _ _ _ _ _ _ _ _ _ _ _ _ _ _ _ _

_____

PHONICS SKILLS

Name _____ Date _____

▶Sounds and Spellings

PHONICS SKILLS

Directions: Practice writing o and O. Copy the word. Then, draw two pictures whose names have the /o/ sound.

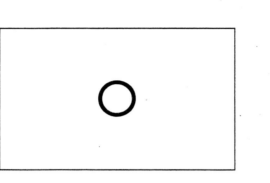

not _____

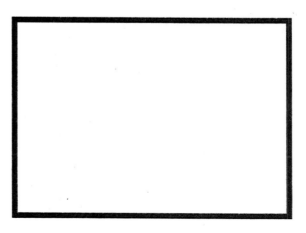

Sounds and Spellings • Reteach: Phonics Skills

▶Completing Sentences

PHONICS SKILLS

Mom has a _____.

pat
pot

Sam did _____.

hop
hip

It is a _____.

map
mop

Name _____ Date _____

▶Sounds and Spellings

Directions: Practice writing *b* and *B*. Copy the word. Then, draw two pictures whose names begin with the /b/ sound.

PHONICS SKILLS

b

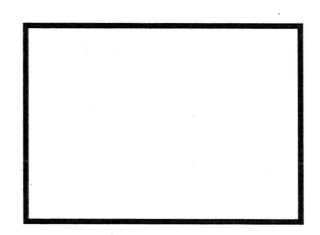

b

B

bat

UNIT 2 Animals • **Lesson 8** *Munch Crunch: Foods That Animals Eat*

▶Decoding

bin
bat

bob
bib

Nan has a bat.
Nan has a bib.

PHONICS SKILLS

_____

- - - - - - - - - - - - - - - - - - -

_____

UNIT 2 **Animals • Lesson 9** *Mice*

▶Sounds and Spellings

Directions: Practice writing c and C. Copy the word. Then, draw two pictures whose names begin with the /k/ sound.

PHONICS SKILLS

c

c

C

can

Name _____ Date _____

► Writing Words

| can | cot | mat | cab |

_____

- -

_____

_____

- -

_____

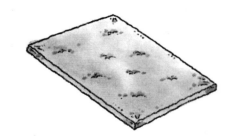

_____

- -

_____

_____

- -

_____

PHONICS SKILLS

_____   cot

- - - - - - - - - - - - - - -   cat

Dan has a _____.

▶Review

PHONICS SKILLS

sand	bin	dots	can

_____

- - - - - - - - - - - - -

_____

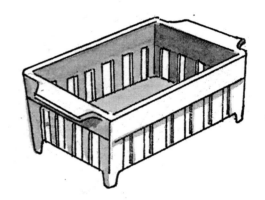

_____

- - - - - - - - - - - - -

_____

_____

- - - - - - - - - - - - -

_____

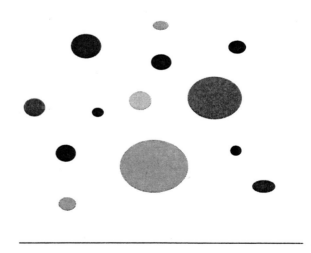

_____

- - - - - - - - - - - - -

_____

UNIT 2 Animals • **Lesson 10** *Spiders*

►Review

PHONICS SKILLS

Nan has a _____.

can
cap

Tim has a _____.

top
tab

Pat has a _____.

dot
pin

Reteach: Phonics Skills • *Review*　　　　　UNIT 2 • Lesson 10　**43**

UNIT 2   Animals • **Lesson II** *Spiders*

Directions: Form words by blending the consonants in the box with _ack, _ick, and _ock.

▶ Sounds and Spellings

PHONICS SKILLS

c

▪ ck

s	t

_ack   _ick   _ock

_____   _____   _____

- - - - - - -   - - - - - - -   - - - - - - -

_____   _____   _____

_____   _____   _____

- - - - - - -   - - - - - - -   - - - - - - -

_____   _____   _____

UNIT 2 Animals • **Lesson II** *Spiders*

▶Reading and Writing

Pam packs the socks.
Mick stacks the sacks.

Dick sits in the back.
Nick sits on the dock.

PHONICS SKILLS

_____

- -

_____

_____

- -

_____

UNIT 2 Animals • **Lesson 12** *The Hermit Crab*

▶Sounds and Spellings

Directions: Practice writing *r* and *R*. Copy the word. Then, draw two pictures whose names begin with the /r/ sound.

PHONICS SKILLS

r

r

R

rat

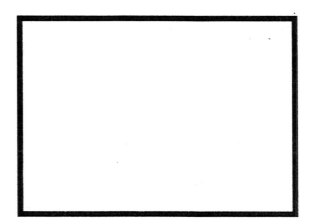

Sounds and Spellings • Reteach: Phonics Skills

UNIT 2 Animals • **Lesson 12** *The Hermit Crab*

▶ Reading and Writing

Ron ran by the rock.
Rick is on the ramp.

The rat sat on a rock.
The ram ran by the man.

Ron rips the sack.
A rabbit hops.

PHONICS SKILLS

_____

- -

_____

UNIT 2 Animals • **Lesson 13** *The Hermit Crab*

▶ Sounds and Spellings

Directions: Practice writing *u* and *U*. Copy the word. Then, draw two pictures whose names have the /u/ sound.

PHONICS SKILLS

u

u

U

run

Sounds and Spellings • Reteach: Phonics Skills

UNIT 2 Animals • **Lesson 13** *The Hermit Crab*

▶ Reading and Writing

Bud is stuck in the mud.
Bud picks up the pup.

A sub is in the tub.
Mud is on the duck.

Pam picks up a cup.
Pam runs for the bus.

PHONICS SKILLS

_____

_ _

_____

UNIT 2 Animals • **Lesson 14** *The Hermit Crab*

▶Sounds and Spellings

Directions: Practice writing *g* and *G*. Copy the word. Then, draw two pictures whose names begin with the /g/ sound.

PHONICS SKILLS

g

g

G

got

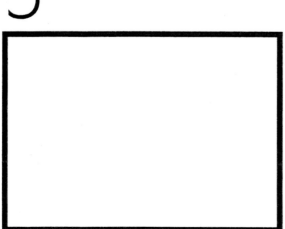

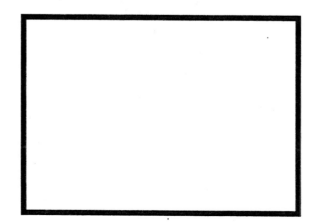

Sounds and Spellings • Reteach: Phonics Skills

UNIT 2 Animals • **Lesson 14** *The Hermit Crab*

▶ Writing Words

bag

rug

tug

gum

dog

big

_____   _____

_ _ _ _ _ _ _ _ _ _   _ _ _ _ _ _ _ _ _ _

_____   _____

PHONICS SKILLS

UNIT 2 · Animals • **Lesson 15** *Unit Wrap-Up*

▶Review

Directions: Look at the pictures. Circle the correct word to finish each sentence. Write the correct word for the last one.

PHONICS SKILLS

Bud has a _____.

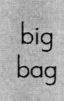
big
bag

Nan tips the _____.

mug
rag

Ron has a _____.

rock
tack

Copyright © SRA/McGraw-Hill. Permission is granted to reproduce this page for classroom use.

UNIT 2 Animals • **Lesson 15** *Unit Wrap-Up*

▶ Review

bun	cat	bin	cut

_____

- - - - - - - - - -

_____

_____

- - - - - - - - - -

_____

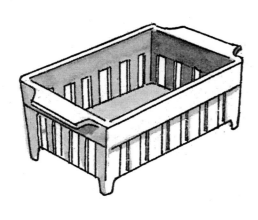

_____

- - - - - - - - - -

_____

_____

- - - - - - - - - -

_____

PHONICS SKILLS

UNIT 3 Things That Go • **Lesson I** *Unit Introduction*

▶Sounds and Spellings

Directions: Practice writing *j* and *J*. Copy the words. Then, draw two pictures whose names begin with the /j/ sound.

PHONICS SKILLS

j

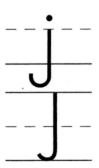dge

j
J

jug   judge

Sounds and Spellings • Reteach: Phonics Skills

▶ Decoding/Dictation

Directions: Read the two sentences, circle the sentence that describes the picture, and write the sentence on the line. Say the name of each picture to the student. Then, have the student write the name of each picture and underline the /j/ spelling.

Jim is a jam judge.
Jan can jog.

_____

- - - - - - - - - - - - - - - - - - -

_____

_____ _____ _____

- - - - - -   - - - - - -   - - - - - -

_____ _____ _____

PHONICS SKILLS

UNIT 3 **Things That Go • Lesson 2** *I Go with My Family to Grandma's*

▶Sounds and Spellings

Directions: Practice writing *f* and *F*. Copy the word. Then, draw two pictures whose names begin with the /f/ sound.

PHONICS SKILLS

f

F

fit

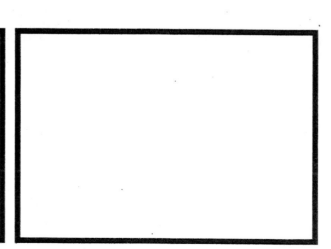

Sounds and Spellings • Reteach: Phonics Skills

UNIT 3 **Things That Go • Lesson 2** *I Go with My Family to Grandma's*

▶ Blending

f i   n

   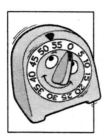

PHONICS SKILLS

UNIT 3 **Things That Go • Lesson 3** *I Go with My Family to Grandma's*

w

▶Sounds and Spellings

Directions: Practice writing e and E. Copy the word. Then, draw two pictures whose names have the /e/ sound.

PHONICS SKILLS

e

e

E

pet

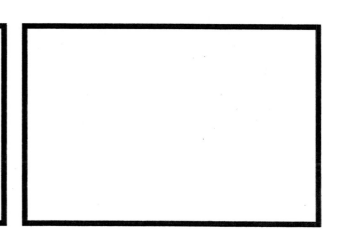

Name _____ Date _____

W

▶ Sounds and Spellings

| pet | tent | bed | neck |

_____
_ _ _ _ _ _ _ _ _ _ _
_____

_____
_ _ _ _ _ _ _ _ _ _ _
_____

_____
_ _ _ _ _ _ _ _ _ _ _
_____

_____
_ _ _ _ _ _ _ _ _ _ _
_____

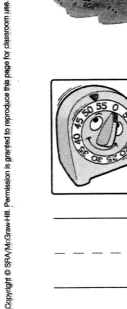      

_____
_ _ _ _ _ _ _ _ _ _ _
_____

_____
_ _ _ _ _ _ _ _ _ _ _

Ted has _____ pens.

UNIT 3 Things That Go • **Lesson 4** *I Go with My Family to Grandma's*

▶Review

Directions: Read the words in the box and name each picture. Then, write the correct word under each picture.

PHONICS SKILLS

| bell | fudge | left | jet |

_____

- - - - - - - - - - - - - - - - -

_____

_____

- - - - - - - - - - - - - - - - -

_____

_____

- - - - - - - - - - - - - - - - -

_____

_____

- - - - - - - - - - - - - - - - -

_____

Review • Reteach: Phonics Skills

UNIT 3 Things That Go • **Lesson 4** *I Go with My Family to Grandma's*

▶ **Review**

Directions: Name each picture and write the correct letter to complete each word.

l	f

_rog

be_t

_og

gi_t

PHONICS SKILLS

UNIT 3 **Things That Go • Lesson 5** *I Go with My Family to Grandma's*

▶ Sounds and Spellings

Directions: Practice writing x and X. Copy the word. Then, draw two pictures whose names end with the /ks/ sound.

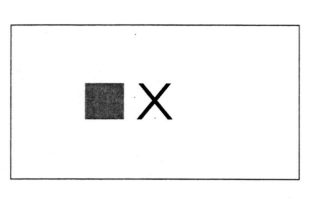

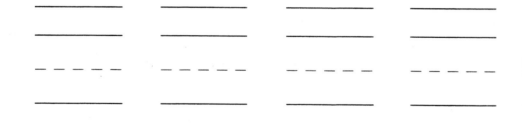

box _____

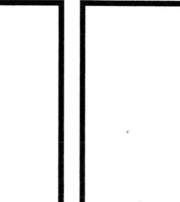

UNIT 3 **Things That Go • Lesson 5** *I Go with My Family to Grandma's*

▶ Listening for Vowels

pod   pad   ox   ax   mitt   mutt

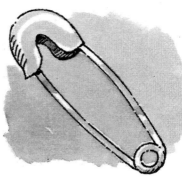

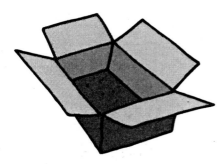

p_n   b_t   b_x

PHONICS SKILLS

UNIT 3 Things That Go • **Lesson 6** *Song of the Train*

▶Sounds and Spellings

PHONICS SKILLS

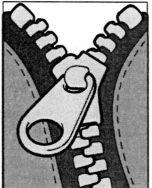

Z
_s

Z
z
Z

zap _____

fuzz _____

his _____

Name _____ Date _____

M

UNIT 3 Things That Go • **Lesson 6** *Song of the Train*

▶ **Possessives**

Directions: Write the correct word for each picture on the left, adding 's to show who has the item pictured on the right. The first one is done for you.

Copyright © SRA/McGraw-Hill. Permission is granted to reproduce this page for classroom use.

| Jan | pig | Tim | dog |

Tim's

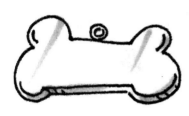

_____

_____

_____

PHONICS SKILLS

Reteach: Phonics Skills • *Possessives*

UNIT 3 • Lesson 6 **65**

UNIT 3 **Things That Go • Lesson 7** *Song of the Train*

▶Review

PHONICS SKILLS

| mix   zip   dress   six |

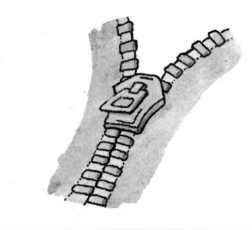

_____

- - - - - - - - - -

_____

_____

- - - - - - - - - -

_____

_____

- - - - - - - - - -

_____

_____

- - - - - - - - - -

_____

Review • Reteach: Phonics Skills

UNIT 3 Things That Go • **Lesson 7** *Song of the Train*

▶ Review

_____

- - - - - - - - - -

Max and Tess have _____ jars.

| grass |
| glass |

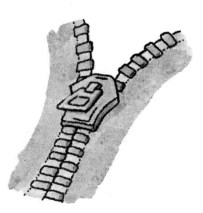

_____   _____   _____

- - - - - - - -   - - - - - - - -   - - - - - - - -

_____   _____   _____

PHONICS SKILLS

Name _____ Date _____

▶Sounds and Spellings

Directions: Practice writing *sh* and *Sh*. Copy the word. Then, draw two pictures whose names begin with the /sh/ sound.

PHONICS SKILLS

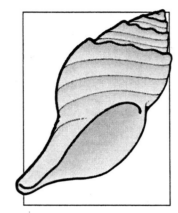

sh

sh
Sh

ship

Sounds and Spellings • Reteach: Phonics Skills

Name _____ Date _____

UNIT 3 **Things That Go • Lesson 8** *On the Go*

▶ Decoding/Blending

| hush | shed | shut | fish |

_____

- - - - - - - - - - - - - -

_____

_____

- - - - - - - - - - - - - -

_____

Directions: Write the correct word under each picture. At the bottom, write the letters represented by each *Sound/Spelling Card* to form a word.

PHONICS SKILLS

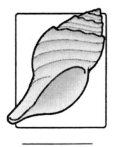   

_____   _____   _____   _____

- - - -   - - - -   - - - -   - - - -

_____   _____   _____   _____

Reteach: Phonics Skills • *Decoding/Blending*   **UNIT 3 • Lesson 8** **69**

Directions: Practice writing *th* and *Th*. Copy the word. Then, draw two pictures whose names begin with the /th/ sound.

UNIT 3 **Things That Go • Lesson 9** *On the Go*

▶Sounds and Spellings

PHONICS SKILLS

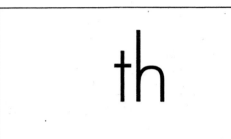

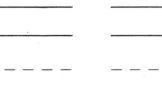

than

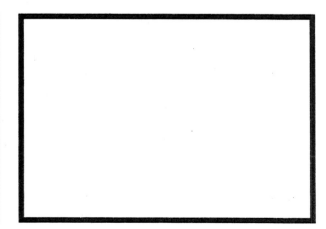

UNIT 3 **Things That Go • Lesson 9** *On the Go*

▶Decoding/Dictation

Directions: Unscramble the words to make a sentence. Write the sentence. Say the name of each picture to the student. Have the student write the name of each picture and underline the /th/ spelling.

PHONICS SKILLS

shell.	Thad	a	has

_____

- -

_____

_____   _____   _____

- - - - - -   - - - - - -   - - - - - -

_____   _____   _____

Name _____ Date _____

▶Review

PHONICS SKILLS

th
sh

 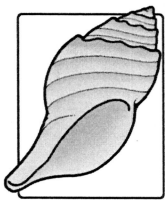

 th
sh

then _____ ship _____

▶ **Review**

Directions: Name each picture. Write *sh* or *th* on the line to complete the word correctly.

sh	th

PHONICS SKILLS

____ick

____op

tra____

$$\begin{array}{r} 1 \\ + 2 \\ \hline 3 \end{array} \qquad \begin{array}{r} 3 \\ + 1 \\ \hline 4 \end{array}$$

ma____

▶ Sounds and Spellings

PHONICS SKILLS

Directions: Practice writing *ch* and *tch*. Copy the words. Then, draw two pictures: one whose name begins with the /ch/ sound and one whose name ends with the /ch/ sound.

ch
tch

ch

tch

chip

itch

UNIT 3 **Things That Go • Lesson 11** *On the Go*

▶ Decoding/Dictation

Directions: Write the correct word under each picture. Say the name of each picture to the student. Have the student write the name of the picture and underline the /ch/ spelling.

hatch	chip	pitch

PHONICS SKILLS

_____

- - - - - - - -

_____

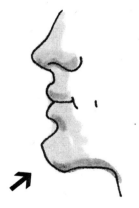

_____

- - - - - - - -

_____

Name _____ Date _____

▶ **Sounds and Spellings**

PHONICS SKILLS

ar

ar ___ ___ ___ ___

___
cart ___

Directions: Practice writing *ar*. Copy the word. Then, draw two pictures whose names have the /ar/ sound.

UNIT 3   **Things That Go • Lesson 12** *On the Go*

▶**Decoding**

PHONICS SKILLS

| arm | card | jar |

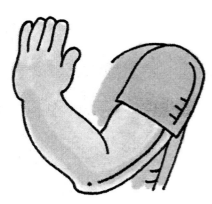

_____ _____ _____

- - - - - - - - - - - - - - - - - - - - - - - - - - - - - -

_____ _____ _____

UNIT 3 **Things That Go • Lesson 13** *Trucks (Camiones)*

▶Review

PHONICS SKILLS

pup	bed	six	pot

Directions: Read the words in the box. Write the correct word under each picture.

_____

- - - - - - - - - -

_____

_____

- - - - - - - - - -

_____

_____

- - - - - - - - - -

_____

_____

- - - - - - - - - -

_____

Review • Reteach: Phonics Skills

▶Review

_____

- - - - - - - - - - -

Lil can _____ .

pitch
catch

_____

- - - - - - - - - - -

_____

_____

- - - - - - - - - - -

_____

_____

- - - - - - - - - - -

_____

PHONICS SKILLS

Name _____ Date _____

▶Sounds and Spellings

Directions: Practice writing w and W. Copy the word. Then, draw two pictures whose names begin with the /w/ sound.

PHONICS SKILLS

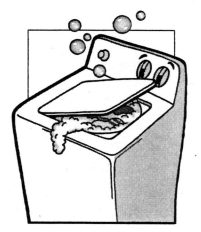

W_

W

W

will

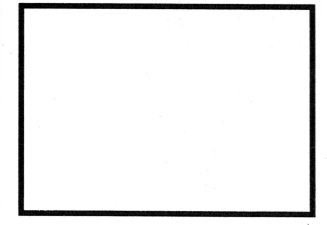

UNIT 3   **Things That Go • Lesson 14** *Trucks (Camiones)*

▷ Sounds and Spellings

wh_

wh

Wh

whip

PHONICS SKILLS

UNIT 3 Things That Go • **Lesson 15** *Unit Wrap-Up*

►Sounds and Spellings

Directions: Practice writing *er*, *ir*, and *ur*. Copy the words. Then, draw one picture whose name has the /er/ sound.

PHONICS SKILLS

er
ir
ur

er

ir

ur

herd

shirt

Sounds and Spellings • **Reteach: Phonics Skills**

UNIT 3 **Things That Go • Lesson 15** *Unit Wrap-Up*

▶ Decoding/Dictation

| bird. | is | her | It |

_____

- -

_____

▶ Dictation

_____ _____ _____

- - - - - - - - - - - - - - - -

_____ _____ _____

PHONICS SKILLS

Name _____ Date _____

▶Review

PHONICS SKILLS

| chin | her | curl | wag |

_____

- - - - - - - - - - - - - - - - - -

_____

_____

- - - - - - - - - - - - - - - - - -

_____

_____

- - - - - - - - - - - - - - - - - -

_____

_____

- - - - - - - - - - - - - - - - - -

_____

Directions: Write the word that goes with each picture.

Copyright © SRA/McGraw-Hill. Permission is granted to reproduce this page for classroom use.

Review • Reteach: Phonics Skills

UNIT 4 **Our Neighborhood at Work • Lesson I** *Unit Introduction*

▶Completing Sentences

PHONICS SKILLS

Bob has a _____.

turtle
bird

Pat sees a _____.

star
car

▶Dictation

_____   _____   _____

_ _ _ _ _ _ _ _   _ _ _ _ _ _ _ _   _ _ _ _ _ _ _ _

_____   _____   _____

UNIT 4 Our Neighborhood at Work • **Lesson 2** *Guess Who?*

▶ Sounds and Spellings

Directions: Practice writing *k* and *K*. Then, copy the words in the spaces provided. Draw two pictures whose names begin with the /k/ sound.

PHONICS SKILLS

k

k

K

dark _ _ _ _ _ _ _ _ _ _ kit _ _ _ _ _ _ _ _ _

Sounds and Spellings • Reteach: Phonics Skills

▶Decoding

Directions: Write the word from the box that goes with each picture.

| kitten | milk | bark | fork |

_____

- - - - - - - - - - - -

_____

_____

- - - - - - - - - - - -

_____

_____

- - - - - - - - - - - -

_____

_____

- - - - - - - - - - - -

_____

PHONICS SKILLS

UNIT 4 Our Neighborhood at Work • **Lesson 3** *Guess Who?*

▶Sounds and Spellings

PHONICS SKILLS

Directions: Practice writing *ng*. Copy the words. Then draw a picture whose name ends with the /ng/ sound.

■ng

- - - - - - - - - - - - - - - - - -

- - - - - - - - - - - - - - - - - -

bring

- - - - - - - - -

ring

- - - - - - - - -

Sounds and Spellings • Reteach: Phonics Skills

▶ Decoding/Dictation

The ring is big.
He sings.

_____

- - - - - - - - - - - - - - - - - -

_____

It has wings.
He swings.

_____

- - - - - - - - - - - - - - - - - -

_____

PHONICS SKILLS

▶ Dictation

_____   _____   _____

- - - - -   - - - - -   - - - - -

_____   _____   _____

UNIT 4 Our Neighborhood at Work • **Lesson 4** *Guess Who?*

▶Sounds and Spellings

PHONICS SKILLS

qu__

qu
Qu

quilt

quit

Sounds and Spellings • Reteach: Phonics Skills

▶ Listening for Words

PHONICS SKILLS

1.

quit   quilt

2.

squint   squirt

3.

A quick squirrel ran.

- -

- -

- -

▶Sounds and Spellings

Directions: Practice writing y and Y. Then, copy the words in the spaces provided. Draw a picture that begins with the /y/ sound.

PHONICS SKILLS

y—

Y
Y

yarn

yell

Sounds and Spellings • Reteach: Phonics Skills

▶Reading Sentences and Writing

The cat bats the yarn.
The man yells in the yard.

_____   _____   _____

- - - - - - - - - -   - - - - - - - - - -   - - - - - - - - - -

_____   _____   _____

PHONICS SKILLS

▶Review

Directions: Write the word from the box that goes with each picture.

| king | yarn | yak | quilt |

PHONICS SKILLS

_____

- - - - - - - - - - - - -

_____

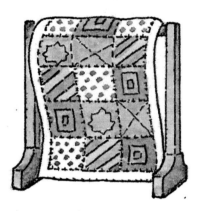

_____

- - - - - - - - - - - - -

_____

_____

- - - - - - - - - - - - -

_____

_____

- - - - - - - - - - - - -

_____

▶Completing Sentences

PHONICS SKILLS

She sang a [long / song] .

Dan has a [skunk / bank] .

The swing set is in the _____ .

[yard / barn]

▶ Sounds and Spellings

PHONICS SKILLS

ate _____

tape _____

_____   _____

_____   _____

UNIT 4 **Our Neighborhood at Work • Lesson 7** *Firefighters*

▶Completing Sentences

1. Pat was _____ for class.

gate
late

2. Sam swam in the _____.

lake
flake

3. Let's play a _____.

game
same

PHONICS SKILLS

▶Dictation

_____ _____ _____

- -

_____ _____ _____

UNIT 4 Our Neighborhood at Work • **Lesson 8** *Firefighters*

▶ Sounds and Spellings

Directions: Practice writing ce and *ci* and copy the words below. Then draw a picture whose name has the /s/ sound spelled ce or *ci___*.

PHONICS SKILLS

s
ce
ci___

_____   _____   _____   _____

_____   _____   _____   _____

_____   _____   _____   _____

_____   _____   _____   _____

race _____

circle _____

UNIT 4 Our Neighborhood at Work • **Lesson 8** *Firefighters*

▶Listening for Consonants

Directions: List each word under the **Sound/Spelling Card** picture for the /s/ sound or /k/ sound.

base	rake	cane	pace

_____

- - - - - - - - - - - - - - -

_____

_____

- - - - - - - - - - - - - - -

_____

PHONICS SKILLS

UNIT 4 Our Neighborhood at Work • **Lesson 9** *Firefighters*

▶Review

Directions: Write the word from the box that goes with each picture.

Copyright © SRA/McGraw-Hill. Permission is granted to reproduce this page for classroom use.

PHONICS SKILLS

tape	cane	gate	ape

_____

- - - - - - - - - - - - - - - - - -

_____

_____

- - - - - - - - - - - - - - - - - -

_____

_____

- - - - - - - - - - - - - - - - - -

_____

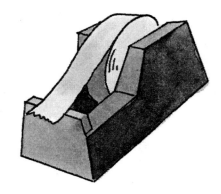

_____

- - - - - - - - - - - - - - - - - -

_____

Review • Reteach: Phonics Skills

▶ Writing Words

f l r

___ace

t c s

___ame

PHONICS SKILLS

▶ Dictation

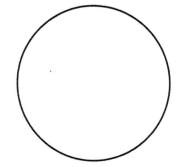

UNIT 4 Our Neighborhood at Work • **Lesson 10** *Firefighters*

▶Sounds and Spellings

PHONICS SKILLS

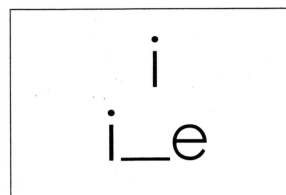

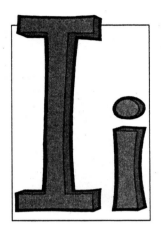

Directions: Copy the words in the spaces provided. Then write other words with the /ī/ sound spelled *i* or *i_e*.

fine _____ pile _____

_____

_____

_____

_____

Sounds and Spellings • Reteach: Phonics Skills

UNIT 4 · **Our Neighborhood at Work** · **Lesson 10** *Firefighters*

▶ Completing Sentences

PHONICS SKILLS

1. The _____ is ripe.

| limp |
| lime |

2. We must stand in _____.

| lane |
| line |

3. Jen rides her _____.

| bike |
| bake |

4. My dog does not _____.

| bit |
| bite |

UNIT 4 Our Neighborhood at Work • **Lesson II** *Worksong*

▶Sounds and Spellings

Directions: Copy the words in the spaces provided. Then write other words with the /ō/ sound spelled o, or o_e.

PHONICS SKILLS

o

o_e

Oo

no ⎯ ⎯ ⎯ ⎯ ⎯   bone ⎯ ⎯ ⎯ ⎯ ⎯

⎯⎯⎯⎯⎯⎯⎯⎯⎯⎯   ⎯⎯⎯⎯⎯⎯⎯⎯⎯⎯

⎯⎯⎯⎯⎯⎯⎯⎯⎯⎯   ⎯⎯⎯⎯⎯⎯⎯⎯⎯⎯

▶ Decoding/Dictation

rope
hope

I ⬚ the sun is out.

stone
hope

Dad can lift a ⬚.

▶ Dictation

_____   _____

\- \- \- \- \- \- \- \- \- \- \- \- \- \- \- \-   \- \- \- \- \- \- \- \- \- \- \- \- \- \- \-

_____   _____

PHONICS SKILLS

Name _____ Date _____

▶Review

lime	rose	rake	plane

PHONICS SKILLS

_____

- - - - - - - - - -

_____

_____

- - - - - - - - - -

_____

_____

- - - - - - - - - -

_____

Review • Reteach: Phonics Skills

▶Review

PHONICS SKILLS

cake
rake

He made a _____.

file
smile

The girl liked to _____.

tone
bone

The dog ate the _____.

UNIT 4 • Our Neighborhood at Work • **Lesson 13** *Worksong*

Directions: Write the word from the box that goes with each picture.
Below, say the name of each picture to the student. Have the student
write the name of each picture and underline the spellings of the
long-vowel sounds.

▶Review

| cane | bone | bike |

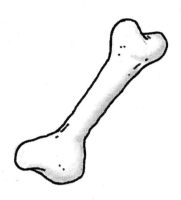

_____ _____ _____

- -

_____ _____ _____

▶Dictation

_____ _____ _____

- -

_____ _____ _____

Name _____ Date _____

▶Review

PHONICS SKILLS

The kitten wore a .

ball
bell

Brett has pet .

mice
rice

Jane ran in a  .

face
race

UNIT 4 Our Neighborhood at Work • **Lesson 14** *Worksong*

▶Sounds and Spellings

Directions: Practice writing v and V. Then, copy the words in the spaces provided. Draw two pictures that begin with the /v/ sound.

Copyright © SRA/McGraw-Hill. Permission is granted to reproduce this page for classroom use.

PHONICS SKILLS

V

vote _____ vane _____

Sounds and Spellings • Reteach: Phonics Skills

▶Completing Sentences

1. Mike **drives** on Vine Lane.

fives	
drives	

2. Viv rides in a _____.

van	
stove	

3. I saved _____ nickels.

hive	
five	

4. Grace put the buds in the _____.

vote	
vase	

PHONICS SKILLS

UNIT 4 Our Neighborhood at Work • **Lesson 15** *Unit Wrap-Up*

▶Sounds and Spellings

Directions: Copy the words in the spaces provided. Then write other words with the /ū/ sound spelled *u* or *u_e*.

PHONICS SKILLS

u
u__e

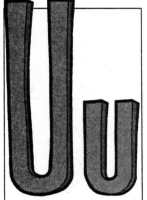

cute _____

cube _____

_____   _____

_____   _____

Sounds and Spellings • Reteach: Phonics Skills

Name _____ Date _____

▶ Reading and Writing

The ice cubes melt.
The mule is cute.

_____

- - - - - - - - - - - - - - - - - -

_____

Directions: Help the student by pointing to each picture and writing it on the line. Say the name of each picture to the student. Have the student write the name of each picture and underline the spelling of the /ū/ sound.

▶ Dictation

_____   _____   _____

- - - - - - - -   - - - - - - - -   - - - - - - - -

_____   _____   _____

PHONICS SKILLS

▶ Sounds and Spellings

PHONICS SKILLS

j

ge

gi

ginger

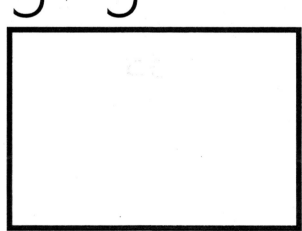

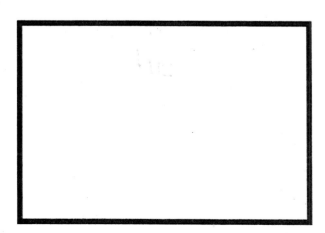

     Sounds and Spellings • Reteach: Phonics Skills

▶Listening for Consonants

| rug | germ | game | stage |

_____

- -

_____

_____

_____ _____ _____

- - - - - - -   - - - - - - -   - - - - - - -

_____ _____ _____

UNIT 5 Weather • **Lesson 2** *When a Storm Comes Up*

▶Sounds and Spellings

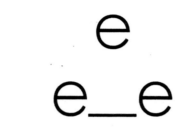

PHONICS SKILLS

me _____

theme _____

she   we

be   he

Name _____ Date _____

▶ Reading and Writing

PHONICS SKILLS

He sang the theme song.
He broke the meter.

She will sit on a bench.
She is an athlete.

We will compete.
We sit on a trapeze.

_____

— — — — — — — — — — — — — — — — — — — —

_____

UNIT 5 Weather • **Lesson 3** *When a Storm Comes Up*

Directions: Read the words in the box. Write the word that goes with each picture.

▶Review

PHONICS SKILLS

| he | vase | cube | stage |

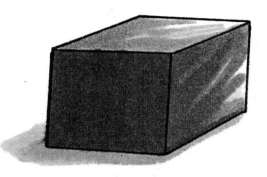

_____

- - - - - - - - - - - - - - - -

_____

_____

- - - - - - - - - - - - - - - -

_____

Review • Reteach: Phonics Skills

UNIT 5 Weather • **Lesson 3** *When a Storm Comes Up*

▶ Decoding/Dictation

Gene has a _____.

mole   mule

The bird is not in the _____.

cage   page

PHONICS SKILLS

she

we

meter

_____   _____   _____

Reteach: Phonics Skills • *Decoding/Dictation*   **UNIT 5 • Lesson 3 119**

▶**Review**

PHONICS SKILLS

| stampede | rice | cane | bugle |

_____

- - - - - - - - - - - - -

_____

_____

- - - - - - - - - - - - -

_____

_____

- - - - - - - - - - - - -

_____

_____

- - - - - - - - - - - - -

_____

Review • Reteach: Phonics Skills

▶Decoding

PHONICS SKILLS

Vince turns the _____.

| hedge |
| page |

_____ can run fast.

| We |
| He |

_____
- - - - - - - - -

Steve has a _____.

| vine |
| van |

UNIT 5 Weather • **Lesson 5** *When a Storm Comes Up*

▶ Sounds and Spellings

Directions: Practice writing ee and ea. Copy the words. Then write other words with the /ē/ sound spelled ee or ea.

ee
ea

PHONICS SKILLS

ee

ea

jeep

tea

Sounds and Spellings • Reteach: Phonics Skills

▶ Writing Opposites/ Dictation

Directions: Read each word in the box. Then, write the correct word on the line next to its opposite. Say the name of each picture to the student. Have the student write the name of each picture and underline the spellings of the /ē/ sound.

PHONICS SKILLS

start	last	fat

first _____

thin _____

stop _____

seal

peach

heel

_____ _____ _____

UNIT 5 **Weather • Lesson 6** *Listen to the Rain*

▶Sounds and Spellings

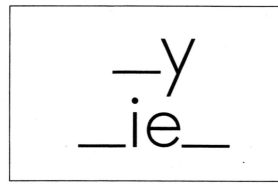

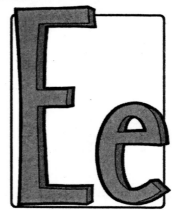

y

ie

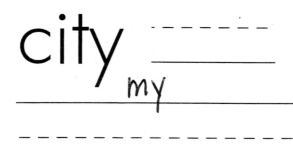

city ___ my

shy

field ___ cry

pie

▶ Decoding

PHONICS SKILLS

The guppies swim in the pond.
The guppy swims in the pond.

Her niece is funny.
Her kitty is funny.

Andy eats a piece of cake.
Andy pats a bunny.

_____

- -

_____

UNIT 5 Weather • **Lesson 7** *How's the Weather?*

▶ Sounds and Spellings

PHONICS SKILLS

| deer | fire | hare | store |

_____

- - - - - - - - - - - - - - -

_____

_____

- - - - - - - - - - - - - - -

_____

UNIT 5 Weather • **Lesson 7** *How's the Weather?*

▶ Decoding/Dictation

The _____ eats grass.

hare   mare

Sam has _____ bugs.

more   sore

_____

- - - - - - - - - - - - - - - - - -

_____

_____

- - - - - - - - - - - - - - - - - -

_____

_____

- - - - - - - - - - - - - - - - - -

_____

_____

- - - - - - - - - - - - - - - - - -

_____

PHONICS SKILLS

Name _____ Date _____

▶Sounds and Spellings

Directions: Practice writing *ai* and *ay*. Copy the words. Then write other words with the /ā/ sound spelled *ai_* or *_ay*.

PHONICS SKILLS

ai_
_ay

Aa

ai _____ _____ _____

ay _____ _____ _____

hay _____ main _____

_____ _____

_____ _____

_____ _____

Sounds and Spellings • Reteach: Phonics Skills

▶Decoding

PHONICS SKILLS

hay   hair

_____

_ _ _ _ _ _ _ _ _ _ _ _ _ _

_____

fair   face

_____

_ _ _ _ _ _ _ _ _ _ _ _ _ _

_____

pair   pail

_____

_ _ _ _ _ _ _ _ _ _ _ _ _ _

_____

stare   stage

_____

_ _ _ _ _ _ _ _ _ _ _ _ _ _

_____

UNIT 5 Weather • **Lesson 9** *How's the Weather?*

▶**Sounds and Spellings**

PHONICS SKILLS

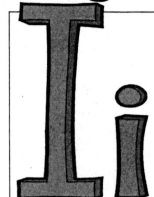

igh

igh

thigh   light

tight   sigh

UNIT 5   Weather • **Lesson 9** *How's the Weather?*

▶ Decoding/Dictation

flash   box

high   light

mail   way

_____

- - - - - - - - - - - - - - - - -

_____

- - - - - - - - - - - - - - - - -

_____

- - - - - - - - - - - - - - - - -

_____

PHONICS SKILLS

_____   _____   _____

- - - - - -   - - - - - -   - - - - - -

_____   _____   _____

UNIT 5 Weather • **Lesson 10** *Clouds, Rain, Snow, and Ice*

Directions: Read the words in the box. Write the word that goes with each picture.

▶Review

PHONICS SKILLS

city	bee	trail	tray

_____

- - - - - - - - - - - - -

_____

_____

- - - - - - - - - - - - -

_____

_____

- - - - - - - - - - - - -

_____

_____

- - - - - - - - - - - - -

_____

Review • Reteach: Phonics Skills

UNIT 5 Weather • **Lesson 10** *Clouds, Rain, Snow, and Ice*

▶Review

PHONICS SKILLS

Lee is _____ with a hammer.

sandy
handy

Tammy has _____ pieces of candy.

thirty
zero

_____

_ _ _ _ _ _ _ _ _

Katie races across the _____.

thief
field

UNIT 5 Weather • **Lesson II** *A Good Day for Kites*

▶Sounds and Spellings

PHONICS SKILLS

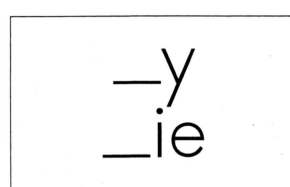

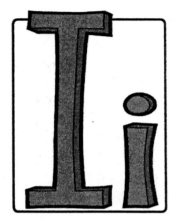

y

ie

fry

tie

Name _____ Date _____

▶ Decoding/Dictation

lie	pie	dries

1. I like apple _____ .

2. Jill _____ her hair.

3. Ty never tells a _____ .

_____   _____   _____

_____   _____   _____

PHONICS SKILLS

Name _____ Date _____

▶ Sounds and Spellings

Directions: Practice writing o and oe. Copy the words. Then write four other words with the /ō/ sound spelled o or _oe.

PHONICS SKILLS

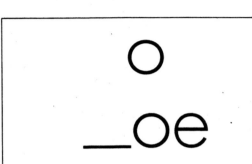

o

_ _ _ _ _ _ _ _ _ _ _ _ _ _ _ _ _ _

o

_ _ _ _ _ _ _ _ _ _ _ _ _ _ _ _ _ _

oe

_ _ _ _ _ _ _ _ _ _ _ _ _ _ _ _ _ _

go _ _ _ _ _ _ _   hoe _ _ _ _ _ _ _

_ _ _ _ _ _ _ _ _ _ _   _ _ _ _ _ _ _ _ _ _ _

_ _ _ _ _ _ _ _ _ _ _   _ _ _ _ _ _ _ _ _ _ _

_ _ _ _ _ _ _ _ _ _ _   _ _ _ _ _ _ _ _ _ _ _

Name _____ Date _____

▶ Decoding

○ home

○ cove

○ dot

○ stove

○ lock

○ hoe

○ go

○ so

○ rose

PHONICS SKILLS

_____
_ _ _ _ _

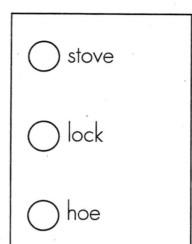

_____
_ _ _ _ _

_____
_ _ _ _ _ _ _

Joe will _____ to get the hoe.

UNIT 5 Weather • **Lesson 13** *Snow Is Good!*

▶Sounds and Spellings

PHONICS SKILLS

o
oa__

oa

boat

road

goat

float

UNIT 5 Weather • **Lesson 13** *Snow Is Good!*

▶ Sounds and Spellings

Directions: Practice writing *ow.* Copy the words. Then write other words with the /ō/ sound spelled *oa_* or *_ow.*

o
_ow

PHONICS SKILLS

ow

mow

grow

▶ Sounds and Spellings

Directions: Practice writing *ew* and *ue*. Copy the words. Then write other words with the /ū/ sound spelled *u_, _ew,* or *_ue.*

Copyright © SRA/McGraw-Hill. Permission is granted to reproduce this page for classroom use.

PHONICS SKILLS

u __ew
__ue

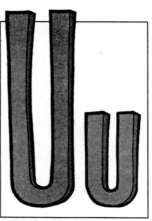

ew ---------- ----------- -----------

ue ---------- ----------- -----------

          _____   _____

pew ---------- cue ----------
    new   clue

---------- _____
              Sue
    few   _____

---------- ----------

▶Decoding

value	rescue	few

_____
- - - - - - -
1. A _____ leaves fell by the birdbath.

_____
- - - - - - -
2. Sally will _____ the card you made.

_____
- - - - - - -
3. Who will _____ the cat in the tree?

PHONICS SKILLS

Reteach: Phonics Skills • *Decoding*   UNIT 5 • Lesson 14   **141**

UNIT 5 Weather • **Lesson I5** *Unit Wrap-Up*

▶Review

PHONICS SKILLS

pie	hoe	goat	pry

_____

- - - - - - - - - - - - - -

_____

_____

- - - - - - - - - - - - - -

_____

_____

- - - - - - - - - - - - - -

_____

_____

- - - - - - - - - - - - - -

_____

Review • Reteach: Phonics Skills

UNIT 5 Weather • **Lesson 15** *Unit Wrap-Up*

▶ Decoding/Dictation

PHONICS SKILLS

Directions: Circle the word that will correctly complete the sentence. Say the name of each picture to the student. Have the student write the name of each picture and underline the spelling of the /ō/ sound.

The campfire will _____.

low
glow

mow

_____

- - - - - - - - - - - -

_____

row

_____

- - - - - - - - - - - -

_____

bow

_____

- - - - - - - - - - - -

_____

UNIT 6 Journeys • **Lesson 1** *Unit Introduction*

▶Sounds and Spellings

Directions: Copy the words in the spaces provided. Then, draw two pictures whose names have the /ōō/ sound.

PHONICS SKILLS

oo   u_e
_ue _ew
    u

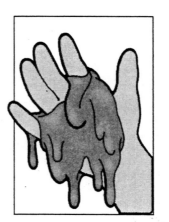

soon _____   rude _____

clue _____   blew _____

Sounds and Spellings • Reteach: Phonics Skills

UNIT 6 Journeys • **Lesson 1** *Unit Introduction*

▶ Decoding/Dictation

1. Dad has a new set of tools.

2. In June Sue went to the zoo.

3. Luke plays the tuba at noon.

PHONICS SKILLS

moon

_____

- - - - - - - - - -

_____

stool

_____

- - - - - - - - - -

_____

tooth

_____

- - - - - - - - - -

_____

Name _____ Date _____

▶Sounds and Spellings

Directions: Practice writing oo. Copy the words. Then draw two pictures whose names have the /oo/ sound.

PHONICS SKILLS

OO

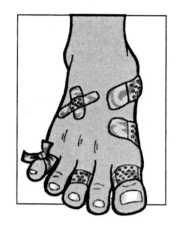

OO _ _ _ _ _ _ _ _ _ _ _ _ _ _ _

look _ _ _ _ _ _ _

wood _ _ _ _ _ _ _

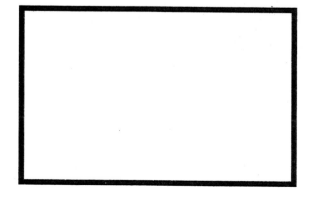

Sounds and Spellings • Reteach: Phonics Skills

▶Decoding

PHONICS SKILLS

Luke has a good book.
Luke stood in line.

Fish splash in a brook.
Fred soaks his foot.

Sam fixes the hook.
Sam stacks wood.

_____

_ _

_____

▶**Review**

Directions: Read the words in the box. Write the correct word under each picture.

Copyright © SRA/McGraw-Hill. Permission is granted to reproduce this page for classroom use.

PHONICS SKILLS

spool	prune	chew	broom

_____
- - - - - - - - - -
_____

_____
- - - - - - - - - -
_____

_____
- - - - - - - - - -
_____

_____
- - - - - - - - - -
_____

Review • **Reteach: Phonics Skills**

▶Review

Directions: Circle the correct word to complete each sentence. Then say the name of each picture below to the students. Have them write the name of each picture and underline the spelling of the /ōō/ sound.

Sue has a _____ vase.

Bob has a _____ shirt.

PHONICS SKILLS

glue
blue

new
chew

plume

_____

- - - - - - - - - - -

_____

stew

_____

- - - - - - - - - - -

_____

boot

_____

- - - - - - - - - - -

_____

Name _____ Date _____

▶ Sounds and Spellings

Directions: Practice writing ow. Copy the words. Then draw two pictures whose names have the /ow/ sound.

ow

ow

down

crown

Sounds and Spellings • **Reteach: Phonics Skills**

UNIT 6 Journeys • **Lesson 4** *Captain Bill Pinkney's Journey*

▶Decoding

now   pow   plow

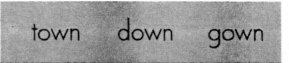

town   down   gown

growl   crowd   howl

howl

_____

- - - - - - - - - - -

_____

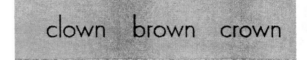

clown   brown   crown

clown

_____

- - - - - - - - - - -

_____

PHONICS SKILLS

▶ **Sounds and Spellings**

PHONICS SKILLS

ou_

ou _____ _____ _____

trout _____

mouth _____

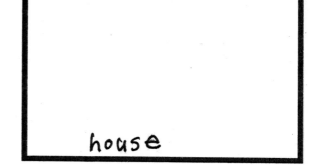

mouse   house

Sounds and Spellings • **Reteach: Phonics Skills**

Directions: Practice writing *ou*. Copy the words. Then draw two pictures whose names have the /ow/ sound.

UNIT 6 Journeys • **Lesson 5** *Captain Bill Pinkney's Journey*

▶ Decoding

Directions: Complete each sentence with the correct word from the box. Then write the words with the /ow/ and /ō/ sounds next to the correct **Sound/Spelling Card**.

row	brown	tow	down

1. This truck will _____ our car.

2. Let's slide _____ this hill.

3. Jill can _____ the boat across the lake.

4. A _____ pup chases the ball.

PHONICS SKILLS

▶Review

Directions: Read the words in the box. Write the correct word under each picture.

PHONICS SKILLS

| cloud | growl | pound | frown |

_____

- - - - - - - - - - -

_____

_____

- - - - - - - - - - -

_____

_____

- - - - - - - - - - -

_____

_____

- - - - - - - - - - -

_____

▶**Review**

Rusty is Grandpa's old hound. One day Grandpa and Rusty walked down to the pond. Rusty had his bone in his mouth. He dropped the bone. He howled and started to dig in the ground. Rusty dug until there was a mound of dirt beside the hole. He put his bone in the hole. Then they finished the walk.

PHONICS SKILLS

_____   _____
_ _ _ _ _ _ _ _ _ _ _ _ _   _ _ _ _ _ _ _ _ _ _ _ _ _
_____   _____

ou_   ow

_____   _____
_ _ _ _ _ _ _ _ _ _ _ _ _   _ _ _ _ _ _ _ _ _ _ _ _ _
_____
_ _ _ _ _ _ _ _ _ _ _ _ _
_____

UNIT 6 Journeys • **Lesson 7** *Me on the Map*

▶Sounds and Spellings

Copyright © SRA/McGraw-Hill. Permission is granted to reproduce this page for classroom use.

PHONICS SKILLS

aw
au_

aw

au

law sauce

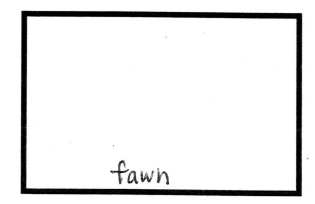

saw

fawn

Sounds and Spellings • **Reteach: Phonics Skills**

UNIT 6 Journeys • **Lesson 7** *Me on the Map*

▶ Decoding/Dictation

Dad put the salt in the _____.

sauce
fault

The _____ swooped down.

flaw
hawk

PHONICS SKILLS

saw

fawn

haul

Reteach: Phonics Skills • *Decoding/Dictation*

▶Review

Directions: Look at each picture and read the two sentences. Circle the sentence that goes with the picture and write the last correct sentence.

PHONICS SKILLS

Ellie has a gown for her mom.
Ellie has a crown for her mom.

Eddie sat in the straw.
Eddie sees the fawn.

Candy draws a hawk.
Candy uses a saw.

_____

- - - - - - - - - - - - - - - - - -

_____

▶Review

PHONICS SKILLS

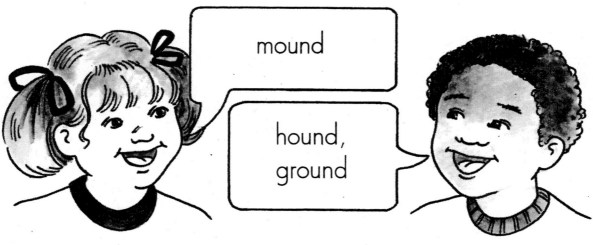

mound

hound, ground

| pound | dawn | sound |

| crow | paw | raw |

| growl | owl | yawn |

UNIT 6   Journeys • **Lesson 9** *Me on the Map*

▶Sounds and Spellings

Directions: Practice writing *kn*. Copy the words. Then say the name of each picture to the students. Have them write the name of each picture and underline the spelling of the /n/ sound.

PHONICS SKILLS

kn_ⁿ

kn _ _ _ _ _ _ _ _ _ _ _ _ _ _

knee _ _ _ _ _ _ knot _ _ _ _ _ _

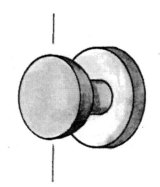

_ _

▶ Decoding

knob	knife	knew

PHONICS SKILLS

_____
- - - - - - - - -

1. Mom cuts the pie with a _____.

_____
- - - - - - - - -

2. Jill _____ how to plant flowers.

_____
- - - - - - - - -

3. Just turn the _____.

Name _____ Date _____

UNIT 6 Journeys • **Lesson 10** *The Plane Trip*

▶**Review**

PHONICS SKILLS

| pool | brook | zoo | foot |

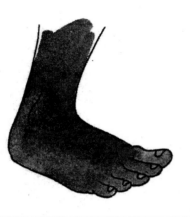

_____

_____

_____

_____

162 UNIT 6 • Lesson 10

Review • Reteach: Phonics Skills

Directions: Read the words in the box. Write the correct word under each picture.

UNIT 6 Journeys • **Lesson 10** *The Plane Trip*

▶Review

_____ at that bright star!

Loom
Look

PHONICS SKILLS

Meg can sit on this ____.

stool
stood

_____

Did you hear an owl _____?

hood
hoot

UNIT 6 Journeys • **Lesson II** *The Special Day*

►Comparative Endings: –er, –est

Directions: Number each set of words in order from 1–3. The first one is done for you.

PHONICS SKILLS

___ longer

___ longest

|__ long

___ smaller

___ small

___ smallest

___ fast

___ fastest

___ faster

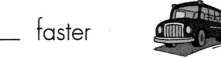

Copyright © SRA/McGraw-Hill. Permission is granted to reproduce this page for classroom use.

UNIT 6 Journeys • **Lesson II** *The Special Day*

▶ Decoding/Dictation

The puppy is the _____ of all.

soft   softer   softest

The blanket is _____ than the sheet.

thick   thicker   thickest

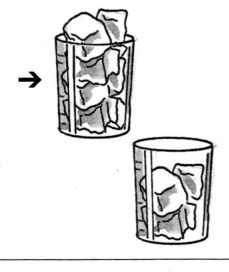

_____

_ _ _ _ _ _ _ _ _ _ _ _ _ _ _ _ _ _ _ _

_____

PHONICS SKILLS

▶Sounds and Spellings

Directions: Practice writing *oi* and *oy*. Copy the words. Then draw two pictures whose names have the /*oi*/ sound.

PHONICS SKILLS

oi
_oy

oi _ _ _ _ _ _ _ _ _ _ _

oy _ _ _ _ _ _ _ _ _ _ _

boy _ _ _ _ _   join _ _ _ _ _

UNIT 6 **Journeys • Lesson 12** *The Library Trip*

▶ Decoding

spoil	hoist	join

_____

1. Mike wants to _____ the team.

_____

2. Bill can _____ the boxes into the truck.

_____

3. The rain did not _____ the picnic.

PHONICS SKILLS

UNIT 6 Journeys • **Lesson 13** *Our Class Trip*

▶ Sounds and Spellings

Directions: Practice writing *wr*. Copy the words. Say the name of each picture for the students. Have them write the name of each picture and underline the spelling of the /r/ sound.

PHONICS SKILLS

r

wr_

wr

wren _____ write _____

▶ Decoding

| wrong | wren | wrestler | wrecker |

PHONICS SKILLS

_____

- - - - - - - - - - - -

_____

_____

- - - - - - - - - - - -

_____

_____

- - - - - - - - - - - -

_____

_____

- - - - - - - - - - - -

_____

▶Sounds and Spellings

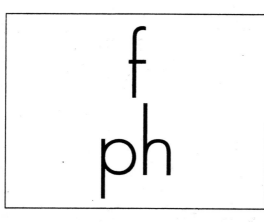

ph

phrase

trophy

Directions: Practice writing *ph*. Copy the words. Then draw two pictures whose names have the /f/ sound.

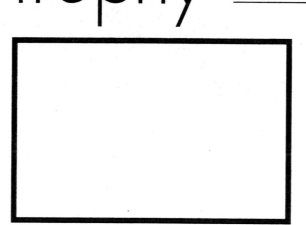

Sounds and Spellings • **Reteach: Phonics Skills**

UNIT 6 Journeys • **Lesson 14** *The Camera Kid*

▶ Decoding

| phone | typhoon | pheasant | photo |

_____

- - - - - - - - - - - - - - -

_____

_____

- - - - - - - - - - - - - - -

_____

_____

- - - - - - - - - - - - - - -

_____

_____

- - - - - - - - - - - - - - -

_____

PHONICS SKILLS

UNIT 6 Journeys • **Lesson 15** *Unit Wrap-Up*

Directions: Read the words in the box. Write the correct word to complete each sentence.

▶Review

PHONICS SKILLS

| wren | coil | choice | gopher |

_____

- - - - - - - - - - -

1. A _____ digs a tunnel under the fence.

_____

- - - - - - - - - - -

2. A worm can _____ into a ball.

_____

- - - - - - - - - - -

3. Bob has a _____ of pie or cake.

_____

- - - - - - - - - - -

4. A tiny _____ chirps in its nest.

Review • **Reteach: Phonics Skills**

UNIT 6 Journeys • **Lesson 15** *Unit Wrap-Up*

▶ Decoding/Dictation

1. race   wren   wrench

2. photo   phrase   fast

3. hoist   joy   moist

PHONICS SKILLS

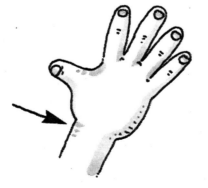

_____   _____   _____

_ _ _ _ _ _ _ _   _ _ _ _ _ _ _ _   _ _ _ _ _ _ _ _

_____   _____   _____

▶Short Vowel Sounds

▶Circle the words with short vowel sounds. Write them under the picture with the same sound.

1. A (bug)(is)(on) the leaf.   3. Kate ate the red apple.

2. Ted saw a fish.   4. The cat runs by the rock.

_____ _____ __is_____

____on_____ ____bug_____

PHONICS SKILLS

UNIT 7 Keep Trying • **Lesson 2** *The Itsy Bitsy Spider*

▶ Long Vowel Sounds

▶ **Circle the words with long vowel sounds. Write them under the correct picture.**

1. Dad (made) a (cute) box.   3. The dog likes to eat bones.

2. Tess will need a pail.   4. Tad will use a light and a rope.

made
_____

_____

_____

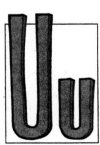

_____

cute
_____

PHONICS SKILLS

▶*o* **Other than Short/Long** *o*

▶**Write the correct word in each space.**

one	above	coming	dove	another

1. She is the <u>one</u> with the green hat.

2. Look _____ the door for the number.

3. The white _____ flew away.

4. Dale is _____ home today.

5. Do you have _____ book?

o Other than Short/Long o • Reteach: Phonics Skills

UNIT 7 Keep Trying • **Lesson 5** *The Way of an Ant*

▶*o* **Other than Short/Long o**

▶ **Circle the correct word. Write it in the space.**

1. I like  _some_ of the animals at the zoo.

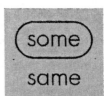
some
same

2. Do you _____ why the sky is blue?

winter
wonder

3. The trip is on _____.

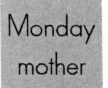
Monday
mother

4. Tad _____ the golf game.

won
went

5. When will you be _____?

don't
done

PHONICS SKILLS

▶ -alk and -all

▶ **Write *alk*. Match each word with the correct picture.**

1. w alk

2. ch _____

3. t _____

▶ **Write *all*. Match each word with the correct picture.**

1. b _____

2. t

3. f _____

-alk *and* -all • **Reteach: Phonics Skills**

UNIT 7 Keep Trying • **Lesson 7** *The Hare and the Tortoise*

▶ -alk and -all

▶ **Circle the correct word. Write it in the space.**

1. Jane had a  __small__ cut on her hand.

   (small) stall

2. We got ice cream at the _____.

   malt mall

3. The _____ broke when the plant fell.

   stalk stall

4. Can we take the dog for a _____?

   wall walk

5. Rob shut the gate to the horse's _____.

   stall small

PHONICS SKILLS

UNIT 7 Keep Trying • **Lesson 8** *74th Street*

▶ o͞o and ū

▶ **Write *oo* or *u* to complete each word.**

m_u_sic

b____m

st____l

men____

r____ts

b____gle

o͞o *and* ū • Reteach: Phonics Skills

UNIT 7   **Keep Trying • Lesson 8** *74th Street*

▶ o͞o and u̅

▶ **Circle the word that is spelled correctly.**
  Write it in the space.

1. Please fill the ice __cube__ tray.

   (cube)   coob

2. A lot of _____ was on the table.

   fude   food

3. We like to ride our _____.

   mool   mule

4. Do you know where your _____ is?

   room   rume

5. Harry dropped his _____ in his milk.

   spune   spoon

PHONICS SKILLS

UNIT 8 Games • **Lesson I** *Unit Introduction*

▶ /aw/ Spelled *augh*, *au_*

▶ Write *au*. Then write the word in the space.

PHONICS SKILLS

1. bec <u>au</u> se

because

2. s ___ ce

3. v ___ lt

▶ Write *augh*. Then write the word in the space.

1. c ___ t

2. d ___ ter

3. t ___ t

/aw/ Spelled augh, au_ • Reteach: Phonics Skills

UNIT 8 Games • **Lesson I** *Unit Introduction*

▶ /aw/ Spelled augh, au_

▶ **Circle the word spelled correctly.**
   Write it in the space.

1. The dog __caught__ the ball.

   cot (caught)

2. The cat drank from the _____ of milk.

   saucer   soser

3. Dad did the _____ today.

   londry   laundry

4. The play got loud _____.

   aplose   applause

5. She _____ the class how to make yogurt.

   taught   tat

PHONICS SKILLS

UNIT 8 Games • **Lesson 4** *Mary Mack*

▶/j/ and /g/

PHONICS SKILLS

▶**Read the paragraph. Write the underlined words under the correct picture.**

Grace's Zoo

Grace's bedroom looks like a zoo. She has a giant gerbil in a cage. On her desk is a tank of ten goldfish. She also got a gentle bird as a gift from her mom. Grace likes to be a zookeeper.

giant _____

/j/ and /g/ • Reteach: Phonics Skills

UNIT 8 Games • **Lesson 4** *Mary Mack*

▶/j/ and /g/

PHONICS SKILLS

Grace's

UNIT 8 Games • **Lesson 7** *The Big Team Relay Race*

▶ Special Spelling Patterns *wa, mb*

▶ Write the correct word in each space.

1. Is the __lamb__ with its mother?

    lamb   yam

2. Did you _____ your hands?

    wish   wash

3. The bird ate the _____ of food.

    crunch   crumb

4. I want to have a glass of _____.

    water   waiter

▶Special Spelling Patterns wa, mb

▶Circle the sentence that goes with each picture.
Write the last sentence on the line.

Mom gave Ben a new wallet.

Mom gave Ben a new watch.

The cat has a limp.

The cat is on the limb.

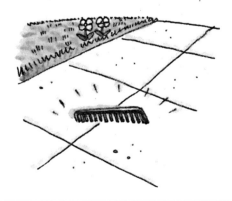

The comb is on the sidewalk.

The cone is on the sidewalk.

_____

_ _

_____

UNIT 8   *Games* • **Lesson 8** *Unit Wrap-Up*

▶/ī/ Spellings

PHONICS SKILLS

▶ **Circle the words with the long *i* sound. Write each word one time in the spaces.**

One (night) Heather and Kate stayed

in a white tent. They had a campfire. It

made a bright glow. Soon the girls went to

sleep.

night _____

   /ī/ Spellings • **Reteach: Phonics Skills**

UNIT 8 Games • **Lesson 8** *Unit Wrap-Up*

▶ /e/ Spelled _ea_

▶**Write the words that rhyme.**

| weather | dread | leather | steady | ahead |

feather ‾weather‾ _____

bread _____ _____

ready _____

PHONICS SKILLS

▶/ū/ Spellings

PHONICS SKILLS

▶ **Circle the words with the long *u* sound. Write each word one time in the spaces.**

Bobby plays (music) on his bugle. He can play a few happy songs to amuse his mom and dad. Bobby wants to be in a huge band and wear a uniform when he gets older.

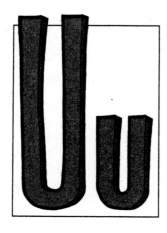

music

_____

/ū/ Spellings • Reteach: Phonics Skills

▶/ū/ Spellings

▶**Circle the word that completes each sentence.**

1. Do they have the (cure cute) for a cold?

2. How much (fuel fuse) is left in the boat?

3. I can make a (cute cube) out of paper.

4. Jackie likes all kinds of (music muddy).

5. The (mule mile) walked up the path.

PHONICS SKILLS

UNIT 9 Being Afraid • **Lesson 9** *Something Is There*

▶/oo/ and /o͞o/

▶ **Circle the words with the same vowel sounds as foot or goo. List each word one time below the correct picture.**

Steve's Loose Tooth

Steve lost his loose tooth when he stubbed his foot and fell at the zoo. He took the tooth home. His mom looked at the tooth. Steve put the tooth in a little wooden box in his room. Soon, Steve will show his tooth to his dad.

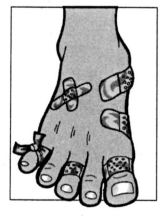

foot

_____

PHONICS SKILLS

UNIT 9 Being Afraid • **Lesson 9** *Something Is There*

▶ /oo/ and /o͞o/

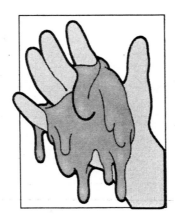

loose

PHONICS SKILLS

►Long Vowels Followed by *r*

PHONICS SKILLS

►Write the word that best completes each sentence.

| share | deer | more | fair |

1. The baby cried for _more_ milk.

2. Will you _____ your books with your brother?

3. The _____ ran out from the woods.

4. The children had fun at the _____ .

UNIT 9 Being Afraid • **Lesson 10** *The Three Billy Goats Gruff*

▶Long Vowels Followed by *r*

▶ Circle the sentence that matches each picture.
Write the last sentence on the line.

Chase has a sore leg.

Chase has a store leg.

Misty goes to the store.

Misty goes to the shore.

Ed drew a pickle of his dog.

Ed drew a picture of his dog.

_____

_ _

_____

PHONICS SKILLS

Reteach: Phonics Skills • *Long Vowels Followed by* r   UNIT 9 • Lesson 10 **195**

▶Vowel Spellings in Syllables

PHONICS SKILLS

▶**Write the word that best completes each sentence. The first one has been done for you.**

| dinner | rattle | bugle | Summer | handle |

1. The baby grabbed the <u>rattle</u>.

2. The man blew the _____ each morning.

3. We had ham sandwiches for _____.

4. The _____ came off the broom.

5. _____ is the best time of the year.

Vowel Spellings in Syllables • **Reteach: Phonics Skills**

UNIT 10 Homes • **Lesson I** *Unit Introduction*

▶ Soft *g* and *c*

▶ **Write the words that rhyme. The first one has been done for you.**

nice	hedge	glance	range
strange	prance	slice	ledge

dance glance _____

ice _____ _____

change _____ _____

edge _____ _____

PHONICS SKILLS

UNIT 10 Homes • **Lesson 7** *Home for a Bunny*

▶ /ē/ Spelled _ey

▶ **Write *ey*. Then write the word in the space. Match it with the correct picture. The first one has been done for you.**

1. hon **ey**   honey

2. vall _____   _____

3. mon _____   _____

4. donk _____   _____

5. jock _____   _____

/ē/ Spelled _ey • Reteach: Phonics Skills

UNIT 10 Homes • **Lesson 7** *Home for a Bunny*

▶ /ē/ Spelled _ey

▶ **Circle the word spelled correctly. Write the word in the space.**

1. The __monkey__ jumped into the tree.

   monky (monkey)

2. The _____ player got hurt.

   hockey   hocky

3. The _____ pecked at some grain.

   turky   turkey

4. Do not forget your _____.

   kee   key

5. A _____ is part of your body.

   kidney   kidny

PHONICS SKILLS

UNIT 10 Homes • **Lesson 8** *Is This a House for Hermit Crab?*

►Special Spelling Patterns: –tion, –ion

►**Write *–ion* or *–tion* in each space to complete the word. The first one has been done for you.**

1. My dog is a good compan **ion** for me.

2. That kind of shirt is in fash_____.

3. Mason won the race and was the champ_____.

4. You are getting an educa_____.

5. Don't men_____ the price of the gift.

Name _____ Date _____

▶Special Spelling Patterns: –tion, –ion

▶**Write the words that rhyme. The first one has been done for you.**

| million | location | stallion | motion | rejection |

1. protection   <u>rejection</u>

2. scallion   _____

3. trillion   _____

4. sensation   _____

5. potion   _____

PHONICS SKILLS